MRS
BEETON
PUDDINGS

MRS
BEETON
PUDDINGS

ISABELLA BEETON
& GERARD BAKER

FOREWORD BY DAN LEPARD

For my grandmothers Nora Baker and Elsie Hinch,
who spanned the gap between Isabella and me.

Gerard Baker

This edition published in Great Britain in 2012 by Weidenfeld & Nicolson
Originally published in 2011 by Weidenfeld & Nicolson as part of *Mrs Beeton How to Cook*

1 3 5 7 9 10 8 6 4 2

ISBN 978 0 297 86684 8

The Orion Publishing Group's policy is to use papers that are natural, renewable and recyclable products and made from wood grown in sustainable forests. The logging and manufacturing processes are expected to conform to the environmental regulations of the country of origin.

Printed and bound in Spain

Weidenfeld & Nicolson
The Orion Publishing Group Ltd
Orion House
5 Upper St Martin's Lane
London wc2h 9ea

An Hachette UK Company

www.orionbooks.co.uk

CONTENTS

FOREWORD

In an age where we rely more on frequent supermarket trips than a well-stocked cupboard, Isabella Beeton's recipes serve to remind us how a few basic ingredients – say flour, eggs, sugar, butter, jam – can be simply transformed into utterly comforting puddings. A rich custard thickened with soft white breadcrumbs and topped with the best raspberry preserve and meringue is an easy dessert, made without a complex hunt through the shops for rare ingredients. Whole apples baked to tenderness under a heavily sugar-crusted suet crust, so the juices concentrate during baking to flavour the pastry, becomes a pudding that impresses instantly yet demands little skill or effort to make.

The original recipes that Mrs Beeton collected were little more than sketches, rather than the detailed methods we're used to today. When I started baking, this sparseness would puzzle me, and only now with experience can I fill in the gaps. In this volume, Gerard Baker's recipes remove the doubt from her writing while still inspiring with her flavours and approach. Where her recipe for pastry expects you to mix your flour and other ingredients bravely and directly on your worktop, using your skill to avoid the water and eggs running onto the floor in a mess, Gerard simply suggests you use a mixing bowl or a food processor. In other recipes his adaptations work more deeply, reflecting a modern diet where we're more comfortable avoiding heavier textures in puddings and where we prefer recipes without too much lard and suet. There are many new ideas in the book as well, taking historic recipes and transforming them into dishes that fit with the more relaxed way we eat today.

Most of all, Mrs Beeton's recipes remind us just how adaptable the most simply equipped modern kitchen is. Though devices like hand mixers and microwaves can dramatically cut the time needed, her recipes also prompt us to remember that just using our hands and simple methods are enough to make a pudding to feel utterly proud of. That's really what good cooking is about, and from these recipes first published over 150 years ago you'll get that extra help you want to make your baking even better.

Dan Lepard

THE INIMITABLE MRS BEETON

When Isabella Beeton first published *Beeton's Book of Household Management* in 1861, Britain was changing from a rural society, in which large numbers of people were involved in farming and many grew their own fruit and vegetables at home, to an industrialised one, where the development of modern transport networks, refrigeration and kitchen appliances brought a world of food to our fingertips.

Today, most of us have an image of Mrs Beeton as a matronly figure – brisk, efficient and experienced in the kitchen. In fact, Isabella Beeton was young and recently married, juggling working outside the home with running her household and coping with the demands of a husband and young family. Having worked on it throughout her early twenties, she saw her book published at the age of 25 and died just three years later.

Although she wrote of housekeepers, butlers and valets, her semi-detached in Hatch End was a world away from the big country houses of the preceding century, and although it is likely that she had some help in the kitchen, she almost certainly managed her home and most of the cooking herself. Her book was inspired by an awareness of the challenges faced by women like herself – and with that in mind, she used her position as editor of *The Englishwoman's Domestic Magazine* to pull together the best recipes and advice from a wide range of sources.

She was among the first revolutionary food writers to style recipes in the format that we are familiar with today, setting out clear lists of ingredients and details of time taken, average cost and portions produced (this last being entirely her invention). She also offered notes on how to source the best food for her recipes – placing particular emphasis on such old-fashioned (or, in our eyes, surprisingly modern) ideas as the use of seasonal, local produce and the importance of animal welfare.

It is easy to see why Mrs Beeton's core themes – buy well, cook well and eat well – are as relevant today as they were 150 years ago. Her original book was written with an awareness of household economy that we can take lessons from too. Because we have access to so much so easily, we often forget to consider how to get the most out of each ingredient – yet maximising flavour and nutrient value and minimising waste is as relevant in the twenty-first century as it was in 1861.

The right ingredients

Mrs Beeton's original recipes have needed careful adaptation. In some cases, the modern recipes are amalgamations of more than one Beeton recipe or suggestion, which I hope give a more coherent whole. Many of the ingredients that may seem at first glance universal are so different today from those varieties Isabella would have been familiar with that using them in the original way can give quite different results to those intended. And all those cases where Mrs Beeton advised adding salt or sugar or honey or spices 'to taste' have been pinned down in real quantities, always keeping in mind both flavour and authenticity.

Cooking methods, too, were in some cases not replicable and in others simply no longer the best way of achieving the desired results. A significant factor in this is that the domestic oven was in its infancy in 1861, and Mrs Beeton was not able to make full use of it in her book. Most kitchens would instead have been equipped with old-fashioned ranges, and there is much mention of setting things before the fire, turning and basting. Baking or roasting, which we now consider simple processes, required constant attention 150 years ago. Oven temperatures, therefore, have all had to be deduced from a mixture of reading between the lines, comparing modern recipes, and testing, testing, testing.

The end result, however, has been to produce dishes that Mrs Beeton would, hopefully, have been happy to call her own.

The legacy

After Isabella Beeton died early in 1865, her book took on a life of its own. It was endlessly enlarged, modern recipes were added and eventually, in the many, many editions of the book that have been published in the past 150 years, the spirit of the original was lost.

The picture of British food that Isabella painted in the first edition was about to change wholesale, and her book was destined to change with it. The aim of this collection is to reverse those changes: to return to real, wholesome, traditional British food, which Mrs Beeton might be proud to recognise as her own – and to put to rest the matronly image.

INTRODUCTION

From the lightest lemon posset to a luscious trifle with its complex layering, puddings are the most delicious ways to end a meal. They should strike a balance between sheer decadence and perfect good taste, and each should fit its occasion. Choose a pudding well, and make it expertly, and your meals will be legendary among your friends and family.

A chilled dessert is lovely at the end of a summer lunch or dinner, and because the British summer provides us with such great berries, one need look no further than a posset or cremet, or perhaps a custard to accompany macerated strawberries or raspberries. Fruit jellies offer an excellent, light-handed way of making vibrantly fresh desserts to round off a rich meal. The two given here (see pages 14 and 16) will be a revelation to anyone who makes them.

Of course cold puddings are not limited only to the months of summer. Poached autumn fruits such as pears, or winter fruit, such as rhubarb, make delicious accompaniments to a serving of homemade cream cheese (see page 82). Seville oranges are a truly seasonal fruit, and only available in the depths of winter. But don't just save them for marmalade. The zest is delicious and can be used to scent custards wonderfully (see page 72).

On a cold day, the rich, seductive aroma of a chocolate soufflé (see page 56) or the nutmeg-scented fragrance of a rice pudding (see page 48) heralds the arrival of perfect comfort food. Many of the traditional hot puddings in this book are mixtures of flour, suet and fruit that have been bound together in a cloth and then boiled or steamed. Serve these in warmed bowls, preferably with Jersey cream or custard (see pages 73 and 74).

Fruit is an incredibly versatile choice, and Mrs Beeton used it widely in puddings, desserts and heavenly homemade drinks. In addition, many of the simple creams and custards in this book are delicious served with fresh or poached fruit alongside. Choose whatever is in season (see opposite) and cook it lightly with a little sugar and lemon or orange juice.

Isabella Beeton was not an expressive or indulgent cook, whatever her reputation might suggest. Her cakes contained rather more flour and less sugar and butter than ours today, but it isn't difficult to work out why. Isabella was a young woman running a household on limited resources. Clearly, money was not in plentiful supply. Nonetheless, she was keen to name butter as her fat of choice for baking – expensive as it was – and this sets a good example for us today.

Whatever you bake, your results will only be as good as the cheapest ingredient you use, so always aim high and buy the best ingredients you can afford. If you only allow yourself one pudding a week, you will want to make absolutely sure it is a very good pudding. And the best way to ensure that it is the best pudding ever is to have made it yourself.

A Seasonal Guide to Fruit

Even in Mrs Beeton's time, gardeners were in the habit of forcing fruits into early cropping inside heated greenhouses, or holding back grapes in storage, their cut stems held in charcoal water. Indoor growing is big business today and has extended the seasons of many of our most popular fruits significantly – yet the availability of fresh, locally grown fruits can still change rapidly. Some, such as strawberries or Seville oranges, have a very limited season and it is worth knowing when to expect them.

Here is a rough guide to seasonal UK produce and major European crops, but since the crops can vary with latitude, altitude and local microclimates it is always worth talking to your local producers and suppliers and asking them which fruits will be the next to appear. Tropical fruits have not been included, as they tend to be available year-round.

January
apples, blood oranges, clementines, pears, rhubarb (forced), satsumas, Seville oranges, tangerines

February
apples, blood oranges, pears, rhubarb (forced)

March
apples, blood oranges, pears, rhubarb (outdoor)

April
rhubarb (outdoor)

May
elderflower

June
blackcurrants, blueberries, cherries, elderflower, gooseberries, strawberries, wild raspberries, wild strawberries

July
blackcurrants, black mulberries, bilberries, blueberries, brambles, cherries, cherry plums, gooseberries, loganberries, peaches, raspberries, redcurrants, strawberries, tayberries, whitecurrants, wild raspberries, wild strawberries

August
apricots, black mulberries, bilberries, blueberries, brambles, cherries, cherry plums, discovery apples, gooseberries, greengages, loganberries, peaches, raspberries, redcurrants, strawberries, tayberries, whitecurrants, wild raspberries, wild strawberries

September
bilberries, blueberries, brambles, cherries, cherry plums, damsons, discovery apples, elderberries, gooseberries, greengages, Marjories seedling plums, peaches, raspberries (late season), redcurrants, strawberries, Victoria plums, whitecurrants, wild raspberries, wild strawberries

October
apples, damsons, pears, quince, raspberries (late season), sloe berries

November
apples, pears, quince, raspberries (late season), sloe berries

December
apples, clementines, pears, quince, satsumas, tangerines

JELLIES
& THIRST
QUENCHERS

RASPBERRY JELLY

✳ Serves 4–6 ✳ Preparation time 20 minutes plus dripping overnight ✳ Chilling time 4 hours

Gelatine, as we know it now, was not available to Mrs Beeton, who instead used isinglass, derived from fish. The development of setting agents fuelled a huge increase in the popularity of jellies and set creams, which were popular with adults and children alike.

2kg ripe raspberries, hulled

110g caster sugar
plus extra to taste

1 tsp lemon juice

approx 3 leaves gelatine

special equipment

a square of muslin and 4–6
serving glasses

Place the raspberries in a large stainless steel or ceramic bowl, add 110g caster sugar and mix together. Crush with a potato masher to form a fairly smooth mass.

Leave the berries and sugar to steep for 1 hour then transfer to a jelly bag (or a piece of butter muslin placed in a sieve or colander) set over a large bowl. Do not press on the raspberries or the jelly will not be clear. Cover with a clean cloth and leave in a cool place overnight to allow the raspberry juice to drip through the fabric into the bowl.

This amount of raspberries should yield approximately 500ml juice. If it does not make enough, make up to 500ml with clear apple juice. If you have more than 500ml, you may need to use more gelatine (see page 66).

To complete the jelly, taste the juice in the bowl. Stir in a little more sugar if you like, and add the lemon juice.

Place half of the liquid in a small saucepan over a medium heat. When the juice it is hand hot remove it from the heat.

Soak the gelatine leaves in cold water for 10 minutes until soft. (If you prefer to set the jelly in a mould you will need to use an extra leaf of gelatine for a firmer set.) Drain, and add to the warm raspberry juice liquid, stirring to dissolve. Pour back into the bowl with the other half of the juice and stir to mix. Now pour the raspberry mixture into 4–6 pretty glasses and chill for 4 hours or overnight to set before serving.

STRAWBERRY JELLY

❋ Serves 4 ❋ Preparation time 20 minutes plus dripping overnight ❋ Chilling time overnight

This delightful jelly has a beautiful colour and flavour. Don't be put off by the quantity of strawberries needed, because the pulp can be used in the strawberry water ice recipe on page 18. Combine the two to make a highly refreshing dessert to follow a summer lunch.

2kg ripe strawberries, hulled

110g plus 1–2 tsp caster sugar

1 tsp lemon juice

clear apple juice

approx 4 leaves gelatine

special equipment

a square of muslin and a 500ml jelly mould

Place the strawberries in a large stainless steel or ceramic bowl, add 110g caster sugar and mix together. Crush with a potato masher to form a fairly smooth mass.

Leave the berries and sugar to steep for 1 hour then transfer to a jelly bag (or a piece of muslin placed in a sieve) set over a large bowl. Do not press on the fruit or the juice will not be clear. Cover with a clean cloth, and leave in a cool place overnight to allow the juice to drip through into the bowl.

This amount of strawberries should yield approximately 500ml juice. If it does not make enough, make up to 500ml with clear apple juice. If you have more than 500ml, you may need to use more gelatine (see page 66). Stir the lemon juice into the strawberry juice and then add 1–2 tsp caster sugar to taste, stirring to dissolve.

Place the sheets of gelatine into a bowl of cold water and leave to soak for 10 minutes. (If you prefer to serve the jelly in individual glasses, and do not intend to turn it out, you can use just 3 leaves of gelatine per 500ml juice instead of 4.) Pour half of the strawberry juice into a small pan over a low heat. When the juice is hand hot remove it from the heat. Squeeze the gelatine sheets to remove excess water and add them to the warm juice, stirring to dissolve. Pour the juice and gelatine mixture into the bowl with the rest of the strawberry juice and stir to mix well.

Strain the mixture through a fine sieve into the mould and chill overnight to set. Turn the jelly out by dipping the mould in boiling water for a few seconds to loosen the edges, and serve with the strawberry water ice.

STRAWBERRY WATER ICE

✳ Serves 4-8 ✳ Preparation time 15 minutes ✳ Freezing time 3-4 hours

This richly flavoured and coloured ice is best made with leftover pulp from the jelly recipe, because the pulp has less water content and is consequently thicker and more jellied as a result. If you have some lovely ripe strawberries and want to make it from scratch, use 800g prepared fruit.

pulp of 2kg strawberries
used in jelly recipe
(see page 16)

75g sifted icing sugar, to taste

juice of 1 lemon

Purée the pulp in a jug blender or food processor and pass it through a fine sieve, discarding the seeds left behind. You should be left with approximately 800g smooth pulp.

Place one-third of the pulp in a bowl and add the icing sugar, whisking until all the sugar has dissolved.

Whisk this mixture back into the remaining pulp with half of the lemon juice. Taste and adjust with more lemon juice or icing sugar if necessary. The flavour should be slightly sweeter than you like, because when it is cold it will taste less sweet.

Pour the liquid into a shallow plastic container and place in the freezer. Stir with a fork or flat whisk every half hour, until the mixture starts to freeze. Then, beat every 15 minutes until it holds a soft shape. Pile into small glasses and serve with strawberry jelly if you like.

If you decide to keep the water ice to eat another day, simply cover the plastic container and leave in the freezer for up to 1 month. When ready to use, place in the fridge for 30 minutes to soften, then beat well to loosen it just before serving.

BLACKCURRANT CORDIAL

✳ Makes approx 400ml ✳ Preparation time 10 minutes plus 24 hours dripping

No other fruit has a flavour as intense as the blackcurrant, making it ideal for a refreshing cordial. Freeze any glut of berries in the summer and you can make this throughout the winter – it is better to use previously frozen fruit as it releases its juice more readily than fresh. If you have fresh fruit, put it in the freezer overnight before using. This is also lovely mixed with English sparkling wine for a more grown-up drink. The blackcurrant pulp left over when you drip the juice can be used to make the blackcurrant cheese on page 82.

800g very ripe blackcurrants, frozen and thawed and picked over to remove leaves and stalks

300g caster sugar, plus up to 100g extra to taste

special equipment

a jelly bag or a sieve lined with muslin

Place the blackcurrants and the sugar in the jug of a blender and purée. Transfer to a jelly bag, or a sieve lined with muslin, suspended over a deep large bowl to catch the drips. Cover everything with a sheet or cloth and leave to drip overnight.

The next day, pour the dripped juice in a jug. Either discard the blackcurrant pulp or use it to make blackcurrant cheese. You should end up with approximately 400ml juice. Add a little more caster sugar to taste. If you prefer a more syrupy cordial, add up to 100g of sugar.

Store the cordial in the fridge for up to 7 days or pour it into a resealable container and freeze for up to 1 month. To serve, dilute in the ratio of 1 part cordial to 2 parts water.

LEMONADE

✳ Makes approx 1 litre ✳ Preparation time 10 minutes plus 2 days steeping

Mrs Beeton recommended a beaten egg white or some sherry to improve this lemonade, but it is just perfect as it is. Use the best lemons you can find and, if you cannot get unwaxed ones, scrub them well in warm water before grating the zest off them.

finely grated zest of 2 lemons

juice of 3 lemons

150g caster sugar or 120g mild English honey

Place all the ingredients in a large jug and top up with 1 litre of water. Cover with cling film and leave to steep in a cool place or in the fridge for 2 days, stirring occasionally.

After 2 days, strain the lemonade into a clean jug and store, covered with cling film, in the fridge. Drink within 7 days.

GINGER BEER

✳ Makes 2–2.5 litres ✳ Preparation time 10 minutes, plus 3 days brewing time

This drink is great fun to make but be warned that it must be left to brew for three days before serving. The addition of yeast makes the beer fizzy so it must be stored in bottles able to withstand high pressure. These are widely available from home-brew shops. To serve, you can add a little extra sugar to Mrs Beeton's original recipe if you have a sweet tooth, or drink it straight up, just as she intended, for a dry, refreshing draught.

80g fresh root ginger, sliced

200g caster sugar, plus extra to serve

¼ tsp cream of tartar

2 lemons, sliced

¼ tbsp fresh yeast

special equipment

home-brewing bottles (3–4 x 750ml or 8–10 x 250ml bottles) and a temperature probe

Place the ginger, sugar, cream of tartar and 200ml cold water in the jug of a liquidiser. Blend until smooth, then pour into a large bowl. Add 2.3 litres boiling water, and the lemon, then cool until it is just warm to the touch, or a temperature probe registers 38°C.

Now place the yeast in a small bowl, stir in a tablespoonful of the liquid and mix to blend. Add this mixture to the remainder of the cooled liquid and leave overnight.

Sterilise the bottles: remove any rubber seals, then place the washed bottles on a baking sheet lined with newspaper and put them in a low oven heated to 120°C/gas mark ½ for half an hour. Place the rubber seals in a small pan of boiling water and simmer for 5 minutes, then allow them to air dry on a tray covered with a clean cloth.

Leave the bottles in the oven to cool, then replace the seals and seal until you are ready to fill them.

Strain the mixture through a fine sieve into a large jug and decant into the bottles. Wrap each bottle in a few layers of newspaper and stand them in a bucket covered with a towel in case of an explosion. Store them at room temperature.

After 3 days place the bucket in a sink, lift off the towel and unwrap and open as many bottles as you need. To serve, place ½ tsp caster sugar in the bottom of each glass, add a few ice cubes and top up with the beer. The beer will keep for up to 1 month in a cool, dark place.

FRUITY
DESSERTS

STEAMED BLACKCURRANT PUDDING

✳ Serves 6 ✳ Preparation time 20 minutes plus 10 minutes resting time ✳ Cooking time 3 hours

Mrs Beeton's recipe for a blackcurrant, or gooseberry, pudding steamed in a suet crust may sound formidable, but this is a splendid thing – steaming, vivid purple with the juice from the fruits, and with an intensity of flavour you will rarely find.

butter, for greasing

¾ quantity suet pastry
(see page 42)

for the filling

400g fresh or frozen blackcurrants,
picked weight

150g caster sugar

special equipment

a 2-litre pudding basin and a
pastry cutter or muffin ring

Grease the pudding basin and set aside. Make the suet pastry and leave it to rest for 10 minutes. Roll out two-thirds of the pastry and use it to line the pudding basin. Roll out the remainder to make the lid.

Thoroughly combine the fruit and sugar in a bowl. Transfer the mixture into the dough-lined pudding basin.

Wet the top edge of the pastry, and place the lid on. Gently seal the edges and trim off any excess pastry.

Take a large piece of greaseproof paper and pleat it down the centre to allow room for expansion during steaming. Cover the top of the pudding with this and then a pleated layer of foil and secure with kitchen string around the edge of the basin, leaving some extra string to make a handle for lifting the pudding basin.

Fill the kettle with water and bring to a boil. Place a pastry cutter or muffin ring in the bottom of a 4-litre pan and set it on the hob. Set the pudding basin on the ring in the bottom of the pan (this ensures that the basin does not crack) and add boiling water to a depth of 15cm. Turn the heat under the pan to medium and bring the water to a simmer. Continue simmering over low heat for 3 hours, topping up with boiling water as necessary.

After 3 hours, lift the basin out of the pot and remove the paper and lid. Turn the pastry out of the basin onto a dish. Serve with custard (see pages 73 and 74) or Jersey cream.

CHERRY CLAFOUTIS

✳ Serves 4 ✳ Preparation time 15 minutes plus 30 minutes resting time
✳ Cooking time 20–25 minutes plus 10 minutes cooling time

A clafoutis, or batter pudding, can be made with any tart fruit, but cherries are the classic. Mrs Beeton used currants in winter, but recommended damsons, plums, apricots or gooseberries in season – showing just how flexible this dish can be. The stones of the cherries are left in here because they impart a subtle almond flavour to the finished clafoutis. Warn your guests to go gently, though, because they will encounter stones in the pudding.

400g ripe cherries, stems removed

80g caster sugar

2 large eggs

200ml milk

100g plain flour

pinch salt

5g unsalted butter

icing sugar, for dusting

special equipment

a 25cm ovenproof frying pan

Place the cherries in a bowl with 40g of the sugar, stir to mix and set aside.

Place the eggs in another bowl and whisk for a minute or two until frothy. Add the milk and whisk again to combine. Sift the flour, salt and remaining 40g sugar into a third bowl and make a well in the centre. Pour in the egg and milk mixture and whisk to combine into a smooth batter. Set aside to rest for half an hour.

Preheat the oven to 180°C/gas mark 4.

Heat a 25cm ovenproof frying pan over a medium heat and add the butter. When it begins to foam, add the cherries and any juice to the pan.

Give the batter a stir to fold any foam that has settled on top back into the mixture and pour carefully into the pan. Place into the oven for 20–25 minutes, or until set and golden on top. Allow the clafoutis to cool for 10 minutes before dusting with icing sugar and serving.

GOOSEBERRY FOOL

✳ Serves 4 ✳ Preparation time 10 minutes ✳ Cooking time 10 minutes

We commonly make gooseberry fool with cream these days as opposed to the more liquid form that Mrs Beeton gives with milk. This recipe gives a light fool that will just hold its shape, and which is perfect when eaten with shortbread. Red varieties of gooseberry can be used in place of the green, but you will need to reduce the quantity of sugar to taste.

400g freshly picked green gooseberries, topped and tailed

50g caster sugar, to taste

200ml double cream

shortbread (see page 60), to serve

Place the gooseberries and sugar into a saucepan over a medium heat and simmer gently for about 10 minutes, until the gooseberries break down. Remove from heat and beat with a whisk to break them up further.

Add 1 tsp sugar to the cream and lightly whip. Fold the whipped cream into the mashed gooseberries with a large metal spoon, until just combined.

Spoon the fool into 4 glasses and chill until ready to serve. Offer the gooseberry fool with some shortbread on the side.

PLUM CRUMBLE

✳ Serves 4 ✳ Preparation time 15 minutes ✳ Cooking time 45 minutes

Although the fruit crumble as we know it today is most likely of twentieth-century origin, Mrs Beeton suggested scattering breadcrumbs over at least one of her fruit puddings as an economical alternative to pastry. The recipe below is for a modern crumble topping: light, crisp and perfect for plums – or other fruits such as gooseberries or apples. Just vary the amount of sugar you use, remembering that the fruit will taste slightly sweeter once it's hot.

700g ripe plums, stoned and quartered

50g caster sugar, to taste

for the crumble topping

125g self-raising flour

50g ground almonds

100g unsalted butter

80g caster sugar

special equipment

a 23 x 17cm baking dish

Preheat the oven to 180°C/gas mark 4.

Put the quartered plums into the baking dish, add the sugar and toss to coat. Taste a piece for sweetness and add a little more sugar if required.

Make the crumble topping by placing the flour, almonds, butter and sugar in the bowl of a food processor. Blend until the mixture resembles fine breadcrumbs then pulse the machine until the mixture begins to come together a little. Alternatively, grate the butter into the flour in a large bowl and rub in with your fingers, then add the almonds and sugar.

Spread the crumble evenly over the plums, then lightly smooth the surface. Place the dish on a baking tray to catch any drips and transfer to the oven.

Bake the crumble for 15 minutes, then reduce the heat to 160°C/gas mark 3, and continue cooking for another 30 minutes until the top is golden and the mixture is bubbling. Serve with custard (see pages 73 and 74) or Jersey cream.

BOTTLED PLUMS

✳ Makes 3 x 1-litre Kilner jars ✳ Preparation time 30 minutes ✳ Cooking time approx 1 hour

This is a simple way of preserving plums or other soft fruit for winter use, especially if you do not have a freezer large enough to hold a glut of produce. The temperatures and times given are specific to achieve a product that will not perish, so you will need a sugar thermometer or temperature probe to make this recipe.

2kg purple plums

1kg granulated or caster sugar (you will require 300–400ml syrup for each 1-litre jar, see method)

special equipment

a sugar thermometer or temperature probe and 3 x 1-litre Kilner jars (standard jars not made for preserving are at risk of exploding)

Halve the plums, and remove and discard the stones. Place a large, deep pan of water over a medium heat. The pan must be deep enough to cover the jars when filled.

Make the syrup by heating 2 litres of water in another saucepan and adding the sugar. Bring to the boil, stirring occasionally, and simmer for 2 minutes, then cool to 65°C.

Ensure that the pan of water is at about 40°C, then pack the halved plums into the jars, pushing them in firmly. Pour the hot syrup over the plums, ensuring that there are no air bubbles and filling the jars right up to the brim. Place the seals on top and screw on the lids, tightening them right up and then slackening by a quarter turn.

Place a sheet of newspaper in the bottom of the pan, and then stand the jars into the water, ensuring that they are covered to a depth of at least 50mm.

Turn the heat up and quickly bring the water to a simmer (about 90°C). Adjust the heat as necessary to maintain this temperature for 20 minutes. When you have finished, carefully lift the jars from the hot-water bath and tighten the screw-on lids. Cool, then store in a cool, dark place and use within 1 year.

BAKED APPLE DUMPLINGS

✳ Makes 4 dumplings ✳ Preparation time 30 minutes ✳ Cooking time 35 minutes

This dessert is simple and splendid. The original recipe doesn't include the spices, but who would serve baked apples without a touch of cinnamon and nutmeg today?

1 quantity suet pastry
(see page 42)

for the filling

4 cooking apples,
peeled and cored

80g unsalted butter, melted

4 tbsp caster sugar

½ tsp nutmeg, freshly grated

2 tsp ground cinnamon

for the glaze

1 egg white, beaten with
1 tbsp granulated sugar

granulated sugar, for dredging

Preheat the oven to 200°C/gas mark 6. Line a baking tray with non-stick baking paper.

Make the suet pastry, divide it into four pieces and leave in a cool place to rest while you peel and core the apples. Roll the apples in the melted butter to coat each one.

Mix the sugar, nutmeg and cinnamon in a large basin. Add the prepared apples and gently toss them to coat inside and out with the spice mixture.

Roll each piece of pastry into a round about 3mm thick, and big enough to cover an apple.

Place an apple in centre of each round, dampen the edges of the pastry with cold water and pull together over the apple. Crimp the edges securely. Place each pastry-wrapped apple on the baking tray.

Brush the egg white and sugar glaze all over the pastry, then dredge each apple with additional granulated sugar.

Bake for 10 minutes then reduce the heat to 140°C/gas mark 1 for 25 minutes, until the apples are cooked. Serve with Jersey cream.

CURRANT DUMPLINGS

✳ Serves 4 ✳ Preparation time 15 minutes ✳ Cooking time 1 hour 30 minutes

This recipe is classic Mrs Beeton – simple, economical and delicious. The currants add a note of sweetness while the salted butter and lemon work together beautifully. A wedge of lemon and some salted butter are all you need to serve it with.

225g self-raising flour
110g currants
85g suet
140ml milk

to serve
1 lemon, quartered
cold salted butter

special equipment
4 x 20cm square pieces of butter muslin

Mix all the ingredients together in a bowl and bring together with your hands to form a soft dough. Divide the dough into 4 equal pieces, shaping each one into a dumpling.

Tie each piece loosely in a sheet of butter muslin and secure it with kitchen string. Place a large saucepan of water over a medium heat and bring to simmering point. Carefully place the dumplings into the water, making sure they are submerged and leave them to simmer for 1½ hours. Simmer the pan with the lid on, topping up with boiling water if necessary.

Remove the dumplings from the water using long-handled tongs and carefully unwrap them. Set the dumplings on a plate lined with kitchen paper to dry for 2–3 minutes, and then serve with a wedge of lemon and a knob of butter. Or, if you are making these ahead, leave them in their muslin wrapping and allow them to cool. Just before you are ready to serve the puddings, reheat them in a pan of boiling water for 20 minutes, unwrap, dry and serve as above.

PEARS IN PORT

✳ Serves 4 ✳ Preparation time 5 minutes ✳ Cooking time 35-45 minutes plus 2 hours chilling time

We rarely come across cooking pears today – historically they were grown because they stored well through the winter, while eating pears were more commonly bottled because they do not keep. The combination with port is a classic one, and you can reduce the syrup to the thickness you prefer.

140g caster sugar

6 cloves

6 allspice berries

300ml port

juice of 1 lemon

4 large pears, peeled, halved and cored

Place the sugar, cloves, allspice, port and 600ml water in a saucepan over medium heat and bring to a simmer.

Meanwhile place the lemon juice in a bowl and add the pear halves. Toss the pears in the juice to coat and to stop them going brown.

Transfer the peeled pears and lemon juice into the hot poaching liquid, cover with a lid and simmer very gently for 25-35 minutes until the pears are tender.

Gently transfer the pears from the liquid into a shallow dish large enough to hold them in a single layer. Strain the whole spices from the liquid, return the liquid to the heat and bring to a rapid simmer. Allow the mixture to reduce until you have about 150ml of a syrupy glaze. Pour over the pears, cover with cling film and chill thoroughly, overnight if you like, before serving. This is lovely served with whipped cream and gingernut biscuits.

POACHED RHUBARB

✳ Serves 4 ✳ Preparation time 10 minutes ✳ Cooking time 25 minutes plus 2 hours chilling time

Rhubarb, as Mrs Beeton noted, comes into season just as apples go out, making it the first new crop of spring. This sharp-sweet poached fruit is a welcome change after the heavy desserts of winter. The original book had it encased in a puff pastry tart, but it is just as good served simply with Jersey cream or custard (see pages 73 and 74).

400g fresh rhubarb, trimmed and cut into 2cm pieces

zest and juice of 1 orange

200ml clear apple juice

50–80g caster sugar

special equipment

a ceramic ovenproof dish

Preheat the oven to 150°C/gas mark 2.

Place the rhubarb pieces into a ceramic ovenproof dish that will take the fruit more or less in a single layer.

Place the orange zest and juice and 50g caster sugar in a small saucepan over a high heat and bring to a boil, then pour over the rhubarb in the dish.

Cover with a layer of greaseproof paper and then wrap the dish with foil.

Bake for 10–15 minutes until the rhubarb is tender to the point of a knife. Remove from the oven and carefully pour off the liquid into a small saucepan. Place over a high heat and reduce the liquid to a syrupy glaze, then pour over the fruit. Allow the rhubarb to cool a little, then taste the fruit. If it tastes unduly tart, add more sugar to taste, then place in the fridge until thoroughly chilled before serving.

BAKED &
STEAMED
PUDDINGS

Tips for Perfect Pastry

* Read the recipe through and make sure you have all the materials to hand and at the correct temperature.

* If the flour and fat get warm and sticky when you are mixing them, chill the pastry for 30 minutes to firm the mixture and then proceed as before.

* Always use cold or iced water for mixing.

* Handle pastry gently, using your fingertips to bring the mixture together – remember that you are making pastry not kneading bread dough.

* Work with the pastry in as cool a place as possible, to help keep the ingredients at the optimum temperature.

SUET PASTRY

* Makes approx 600g * Preparation time 10 minutes plus 30 minutes chilling time

This pastry uses self-raising flour, which was not available to Mrs Beeton, but it lightens the resulting pastry considerably and also makes it more absorbent, which is excellent for puddings (such as the steamed blackcurrant pudding on page 26 and the dumplings on pages 34 and 35).

375g self-raising flour
scant 1 tsp salt
130g suet, grated
250ml cold water

Sift the flour and salt into a large bowl and mix in the suet. Add half of the water. Stir well with a fork, working quickly but gently. Using your fingertips, bring the dough together. Add more water as necessary until everything is evenly mixed and there are no dry lumps of flour.

Bring the mixture together into a smooth, supple lump. Carefully form it into a ball, wrap in cling film and chill for 30 minutes before using.

SHORTCRUST PASTRY

✳ Makes enough for 1 x 22–25cm pie ✳ Preparation time 10 minutes plus 1 hour chilling time

Mrs Beeton gives several recipes for short or everyday pastry, varying the proportion of fat to flour depending on the purpose. However, this simple half-fat-to-flour recipe is really all you need ever use. A little lemon juice added to the mix gives a crisper result.

250g plain flour

pinch salt

125g cold unsalted butter, cubed or grated

½ tsp lemon juice

100ml iced water

If you have a food processor, sift the flour and salt into the bowl and mix. Add the cubed butter and pulse until the mixture resembles fine breadcrumbs. Pour the mixture into a bowl.

If you are working by hand, sift the flour and salt into a bowl and add the cubed or grated butter. Rub the butter and flour between your fingertips until it resembles fine breadcrumbs, working quickly to keep the mixture as cool as possible. If it starts to feel sticky, chill the mixture for 30 minutes before moving on to the next step.

Add the lemon juice to the water and pour two-thirds of this into the flour mixture. Blend well with a fork, stirring quickly but gently. Using your fingertips, bring the dough together. Add more water as necessary (you may need to use all of it) until everything is evenly mixed and there are no dry lumps of flour. Bring the mixture together into a smooth, supple lump. Carefully form the pastry into a flattened ball, wrap in cling film and chill for at least 1 hour before using.

BAKED BREAD PUDDING

✳ Makes 12 servings ✳ Preparation time 40 minutes including soaking time ✳ Cooking time 50 minutes

Bread pudding is an enduring classic which, although it was clearly invented as a means of using up old bread, is delicious enough to hold its own among more extravagant, less thrifty desserts. Mrs Beeton's version has a nice mix of citrus and almond and is delicious hot or cold.

350g stale brown bread, crusts removed

40g caster sugar

40g soft brown sugar

70g candied peel

140g sultanas

¼ tsp ground cinnamon

¼ tsp freshly grated nutmeg

450ml milk

$\frac{1}{8}$ tsp almond essence

3 medium eggs

80g unsalted butter, plus extra for greasing

1 tbsp brandy

2 tbsp demerara sugar, for sprinkling

special equipment

a deep 22 x 17cm baking dish

Tear the stale bread into 2cm pieces and place in a large bowl. Add the sugars, candied peel, sultanas and spices and toss gently to mix.

In another bowl beat the milk, almond essence and eggs together and then pour into the bread mixture. Mix well and leave the ingredients to soak for 30 minutes.

Preheat the oven to 160°C/gas mark 3 and butter the baking dish.

Melt the butter in a small saucepan over a high heat until it is foaming, then beat into the bread mixture. Add the brandy and mix well until all the ingredients are combined.

Pour the mixture into the baking dish and sprinkle over the Demerara sugar.

Cook at 160°C/gas mark 3 for 20 minutes then turn the oven down to 150°C/gas mark 2 for 30 minutes until set and golden brown.

Just before the pudding is cooked, preheat the grill to hot. Place the finished pudding under the grill for about 2 minutes, or until the top has caramelised. Serve with plain yoghurt on the side.

BREAD & BUTTER PUDDING

✳ Serves 6 ✳ Preparation time 20 minutes plus 30 mintues soaking time
✳ Cooking time 50 minutes plus 5 minutes resting time

Mrs Beeton recommends grated citrus peel for her bread and butter pudding, but a spoonful or two of marmalade gives a sweeter zing that sets this dish off perfectly. You can vary the richness of the pudding by altering the ratio of cream to milk.

800ml mixed cream and milk, half of each

120g caster sugar

4 medium eggs

4 yolks

75g softened unsalted butter

300g stale sliced bread

75g marmalade (or the grated zest of 1 orange)

25g granulated sugar

special equipment

a 20cm square ovenproof dish and a large roasting tin

Place the mixed milk and cream in a saucepan over a medium heat, add half the sugar and stir. Meanwhile, in a large bowl, beat the eggs and yolks with the remaining sugar until light and fluffy. When the milk mixture reaches simmering, pour it into the egg mixture and beat to amalgamate. Quickly strain it through a sieve into a large, cold bowl and set aside.

Butter the sliced bread and then spread with marmalade. Cut the slices in half and then arrange them overlapping in the ovenproof dish with the crusts uppermost.

Carefully pour the custard over the bread. Leave to stand for 30 minutes, or until all the liquid has been absorbed. Sprinkle over the granulated sugar.

Preheat the oven to 140°C/gas mark 1. Fill the kettle and bring to a boil. Place the ovenproof dish in a large roasting tin. Pour in enough boiling water to come halfway up sides of the dish. Bake for 50 minutes, or until lightly set and golden brown.

Remove from the oven and let the pudding sit for 5 minutes to rest before serving.

QUEEN'S PUDDING

✳ Serves 4–6 ✳ Preparation time 50 minutes ✳ Cooking time 45–55 minutes

Of all the flavoured milk and breadcrumb puddings that crop up in the British repertoire, this one is the best and originates long before Mrs Beeton wrote her book. It is very similar to her Manchester pudding but requires no pastry, so is quicker to make for the time-pressured cook. The lemon-scented base contrasts perfectly with the raspberry jam and light meringue topping.

650ml milk

25g unsalted butter, plus extra for greasing

25g caster sugar

seeds scraped from one vanilla pod

110g stale white bread or cake crumbs

finely grated zest of ½ lemon

pinch freshly grated nutmeg

4 egg yolks

200g sharp raspberry jam

for the meringue topping

6 egg whites

300g caster sugar

special equipment

a deep, 22cm pie dish and a roasting tin

Place the milk, butter, sugar and vanilla seeds in a saucepan over a medium heat and bring almost to simmering. Remove from the heat and leave for the flavour to infuse for 30 minutes.

Preheat the oven to 160°C/gas mark 3. Butter the pie dish.

Place the bread or cake crumbs, lemon zest and nutmeg into a large bowl and combine. Pour in the infused milk and mix together.

Fill the kettle and bring it to a boil.

Lightly beat the egg yolks and add them a little at a time to the bread mixture until fully incorporated. Then pour the mixture into a buttered baking dish and place in a roasting tin.

Pour boiling water into the roasting tin to a depth of 2cm and bake for 35–45 minutes, or until set. Remove from oven and spread the raspberry jam over the base.

Turn the oven up to 200°C/gas mark 6.

Make the meringue topping by placing the egg whites into the bowl of a mixer and beating them quickly for 2 minutes. Add the sugar and beat to make a stiff meringue. Pile this over the layer of jam, spreading the meringue carefully right to the edges of the dish. Bake for 10 minutes, or until the pudding turns golden brown on top. Allow the pudding to cool a little before serving.

BAKED RICE PUDDING

✳ Serves 4 ✳ Preparation time 5 minutes ✳ Cooking time 3 hours including resting time

Mrs Beeton wrote of rice that 'baking it in puddings is the best mode of preparing it'. She had several recipes for rice puddings, most of which were boiled on the stove, but this baked version is fuss-free and can even cook alongside your roast if you have more than one oven. The key to making a good rice pudding is in allowing plenty of time for the rice to cook – and you will note that this dish can seem very liquid up until the final third of the cooking time, when the rice begins to swell.

**500ml whole milk
(Jersey for preference)**

30g caster sugar

15g unsalted butter

50g pudding rice

1 bay leaf (optional)

nutmeg, freshly grated to taste

special equipment

**a 17cm square baking dish,
3–4cm deep**

Preheat the oven to 140°C/gas mark 1.

Place the milk and sugar in a saucepan over a medium heat. Add the butter and stir until the milk is hot and the butter has melted.

Put the rice into the baking dish. Pour over the heated milk mixture, add the bay leaf, if using, and stir well.

Bake for 2½ hours, giving the pudding a stir about every 30 minutes.

Remove from oven and grate a little nutmeg over top. Turn oven up to 160°C/gas mark 3, and return the pudding to the oven for 15 minutes.

Remove the bay leaf, if using, and leave the finished pudding to rest in a warm place for 10 minutes. Serve with warmed jam or bottled fruits (see page 33).

BAKEWELL PUDDING

✳ Serves 6 ✳ Preparation time 20 minutes plus 30 minutes resting time ✳ Cooking time 1 hour 25 minutes

This lovely pudding is one of the treasures of this book. Mrs Beeton used puff pastry for her Bakewell pudding, but a well-baked shortcrust tart case is a better match, giving a crisp contrast to the rich, silky filling. Use homemade raspberry jam if you have it, or choose a sharp conserve to contrast with the sweet filling.

½ quantity shortcrust pastry (see page 43)

for the filling

115g butter

160g caster sugar

30g ground almonds

5 egg yolks and 1 egg white

80g sharp, best-quality raspberry jam

special equipment

a deep 22cm metal pie dish and some baking beans

First make the pastry and leave it to rest in the fridge for 20 minutes. Then, roll the pastry out on a floured surface to a 27cm round. Place it in the pie dish, leaving the extra pastry hanging over the edge. Line the pastry with a large piece of non-stick baking paper and then fill with baking beans. Leave to rest in a cool place for 10 minutes.

Preheat the oven to 200°C/gas mark 6.

Place the pastry case on a baking tray and bake for 35 minutes until firm and golden brown. Remove the beans and paper and return the case to the oven for 5 minutes to bake further and dry slightly. Remove from the oven and set aside. Reduce the oven to 160°C/gas mark 3.

Make the filling by melting the butter in a medium pan over a low heat. Remove from the heat, and add the sugar, ground almonds and eggs, beating well to combine.

Spread the jam into the pastry case and carefully pour over the filling. Bake for 15 minutes, then turn the oven to 140°C/gas mark 1 for a further 30 minutes until the filling is just firm to the touch. Trim the pastry hanging over the rim with a sharp knife and cool to room temperature before serving.

CHRISTMAS PUDDING

✳ Makes 3 x 500g puddings ✳ Preparation time 1 hour
✳ Cooking time 4 hours initial steaming, then 3 hours to reheat

Mrs Beeton gave several recipes for plum and other Christmas puddings; this recipe takes the best elements from each. Only a small amount of egg is used to bind the mixture, resulting in a lighter, fruitier pudding – but it is essential to use high-quality dried fruit.

butter, for greasing

170g extra-large Muscatel (Lexia) raisins

170g currants

170g sultanas

115g dark muscovado sugar

1 tbsp black treacle

225g white breadcrumbs

2 medium eggs

170g grated suet

50g chopped candied peel

zest of ½ lemon, finely grated

¼ tsp freshly grated nutmeg

¼ tsp ground cinnamon

100ml Jubilee Stout or milk, to mix

few drops almond extract

special equipment

3 x 500ml pudding basins and a pastry cutter or muffin ring

Butter the pudding basins well. Mix all of the rest of the ingredients together in a large bowl ensuring that everything is well blended. Divide the mixture between the 3 basins.

Take 3 pieces of greaseproof paper and make a pleat down the centre of each to allow room for expansion during steaming. Cover the top of each pudding with a pleated piece of greaseproof paper followed by a pleated piece of foil and secure by tying kitchen string around the edge of the basin, leaving some extra string to make a handle for lifting the pudding.

If you have a large steamer, steam all of the puddings at once, ensuring that the steamer does not boil dry. Alternatively, steam each pudding in turn, keeping them in the fridge until you are ready to cook them.

If you do not have a steamer, fill the kettle with water and bring to a boil. Place a pastry cutter or muffin ring in the base of a 4-litre pan and put it on the hob. Set 1 of the 3 pudding basins on the ring in the bottom of the pan (this ensures that the basin does not crack) and add boiling water to a depth of 15cm. Turn the heat under the pan to medium and bring the water to a simmer. Continue simmering over low heat for 4 hours, topping up with boiling water as necessary. Steam each pudding in turn.

When the puddings are cold, wrap them in foil and store in a cool dark place for up to 1 year.

TREATS &
TRIFLES

CHOCOLATE SOUFFLE

✳ Serves 4 people ✳ Preparation time 20 minutes ✳ Cooking time 10 minutes

This lovely soufflé is a perfect dinner-party dessert. The flour has been removed from Mrs Beeton's recipe because it is not really necessary; without it, this dish has the advantage of being gluten free. It is delicious served with vanilla ice cream.

to line the ramekins

softened butter, for greasing

1 tsp cocoa powder

1 tsp caster sugar

for the soufflé

80g plain chocolate (65–72% minimum cocoa solids)

3 medium eggs

1 ½ tbsp caster sugar

1 tbsp brandy (optional)

special equipment

4 x 120ml ramekins, a large heatproof bowl and a roasting tin

Preheat the oven to 200°C/gas mark 6.

Butter the ramekins well, taking care to ensure the top edge is buttered to allow the soufflé to rise without sticking. Combine the cocoa powder and sugar together and sprinkle a little of the mixture into each ramekin, rolling it around until the insides are coated. Set the ramekins aside until needed.

Break up the chocolate and place it in a large heatproof bowl set over a pan of barely simmering water, making sure that the bottom of the bowl does not touch the water. Do not stir vigorously, but stir occasionally to make sure that the chocolate does not seize on the bottom of the bowl and go stiff.

Place the eggs and sugar in the bowl of an electric mixer and beat until the mixture is mousse-like and very pale and thick. Alternatively, whisk with an electric handwhisk.

When the chocolate has fully melted, remove it from the heat and fold in one-third of the egg mixture. Then, working quickly and carefully, fold in the remaining egg mixture, along with the brandy, if liked.

Divide the mixture between the ramekins, wiping off any spills. Place them in a roasting tin and add enough boiling water to reach halfway up the sides of the ramekins.

Place in the oven for 10 minutes until risen but still a little soft in the middle and serve immediately.

SPONGE CAKE

✻ Serves 10 ✻ Preparation time 20 minutes ✻ Cooking time 25 minutes

This basic sponge cake recipe can be used, sliced and layered, in a trifle (see opposite) and the crumbs can be used in the queen's pudding on page 46.

25g unsalted butter, melted, plus a little extra for greasing

3 medium eggs

85g caster sugar

½–1 tbsp orange flower water

85g plain flour

20g unsalted butter, melted, plus a little extra for greasing

finely grated zest of ⅓ lemon

115g plain flour, sifted

special equipment

a deep 20cm round cake tin

Preheat the oven to 180°C/gas mark 4. Grease the cake tin with a little soft butter, then line the base with non-stick baking paper.

Using an electric mixer, whisk the eggs for a minute then add the sugar and orange flower water. Beat at high speed for 10–15 minutes until the mixture is light and mousse-like.

Working quickly but gently, fold in the lemon zest and flour, and then the melted butter. Make sure all of the ingredients are well incorporated and there are no lumps.

Pour the batter into the prepared tin and place in the centre of the oven. Bake for 25 minutes or until evenly browned all over. It is cooked when the cake is firm to a light touch and a skewer inserted into the middle comes out clean.

TRIFLE

✳ Serves 6–8 ✳ Preparation time 1 hour 45 minutes split over 3 days

If one dessert sums up the British kitchen, it would probably be the trifle. This recipe is a combination of elements from several of Mrs Beeton's trifle recipes. At a pinch, you can use puréed fresh raspberries to make up the jelly quantities – just sweeten to taste.

sponge cake (see page 58)

600ml raspberry jelly (see page 14)

3 tbsp homemade or sharp raspberry jam

100ml sweet sherry, or more, to taste

1 quantity everyday custard (see page 73)

for the topping

600ml double cream

15g caster sugar

finely grated zest of 1 lemon

45ml Amontillado sherry

special equipment

a large, attractive glass serving bowl

Make the sponge and begin the jelly on the first day, leaving the jelly to drip overnight.

Cut the sponge in half and spread the bottom half with the raspberry jam. Replace the top half and cut the sponge into small rectangles. Take a large glass serving bowl and line it with the sponge rectangles.

Sprinkle the sponge all over with the sherry, then finish the raspberry jelly and pour it over the sponge. Cover with cling film and chill overnight.

On the third day make the custard and set it aside to cool. Remove the trifle bowl from the fridge and peel back the cling film. Pour the custard over the raspberry jelly and smooth the surface with a palette knife. Re-cover with the cling film and store in a cool place until needed.

When you are ready to serve the trifle, remove the cling film and start the topping. Whip the cream with the sugar, lemon zest and sherry until it forms soft peaks, then pile it on top of the custard, spreading it carefully to the edges of the dish.

SHORTBREAD

✳ Makes 30 fingers ✳ Preparation time 10 minutes plus 30 minutes chilling time ✳ Cooking time 50 minutes

Mrs Beeton's original Scotch shortbread recipe contains caraway seeds, finely chopped blanched almonds and candied orange peel. Here, it has been pared back for simplicity, with semolina added for texture instead of the more highly flavoured nuts and seeds, but any or all of the original embellishments can be retained if you like. These are simply the finest biscuits to accompany the creamy puddings and fruit desserts found in this book, though it would be highly satisfying to enjoy one or two with nothing more than a cup of afternoon tea.

250g unsalted butter, diced

120g caster sugar, plus
1 tbsp for dredging

90g fine semolina

370g sifted plain flour

special equipment

a 20cm square baking tin

Beat the butter until it is soft, and then add the sugar, semolina and flour. Knead lightly to combine. Press the dough evenly into the tin then chill for 30 minutes.

Just before you are ready to bake preheat the oven to 150°C/ gas mark 2. Place the shortbread in the centre of the oven for 50 minutes, or until it is an even pale golden-brown colour. Remove from the oven and dredge with the tablespoon of caster sugar. Leave to cool for 10 minutes in the tin, then cut into fingers. When it is completely cold, lift the biscuits out of the tin and place them in an airtight container. These will keep for up to 1 week.

TOFFEE APPLES

✳ Makes 8 ✳ Preparation time 10 minutes ✳ Cooking time 30 minutes plus 10 minutes cooling time

Mrs Beeton gives a recipe for Everton toffee which, with its addition of lemon juice, is crisp and delicious. This recipe can be made into toffee, like hers, or used to wrap around dessert apples – which are great fun for children on bonfire night, or indeed at any other time of year.

8 medium Cox's Orange
Pippin apples

40g salted butter, plus
extra for greasing

350g soft brown sugar

125ml water

1 tsp lemon juice

170g golden syrup

special equipment

8 x 15cm long lolly sticks or pieces
of dowel, some clear cellophane
and a temperature probe

Wash the apples in very hot water to remove any wax and dry well.

Spear the stalk end of each apple with a lolly stick or a piece of dowel. Grease a baking tray and prepare a jug of very cold water large enough to dip an apple into. Set both aside.

Place the rest of the ingredients in a large pan over a medium heat and allow them to melt together and dissolve, then turn the heat to high and bring the mixture to a boil. Stir constantly and use a temperature probe to monitor the temperature. It is ready when it reaches approximately 148°C. If you don't have a temperature probe, test the set by dropping a small spoonful of the mixture into the jug of cold water. When it forms a crisp string of toffee, remove the pan from the heat.

Working quickly before the toffee sets, hold an apple by the stick and dip it into the toffee, swirling it to ensure it is completely covered. Lift it out of the mixture, allow it to drip for a few seconds and then plunge it into the jug of cold water. Leave it there for a minute while you dip the next apple. Remove the first apple from the jug and set it, with the stick pointing upwards, on the buttered baking tray. Repeat the process with the remaining apples. Leave them to cool for 10 minutes then wrap each apple in cellophane or greaseproof paper.

CREAMS &
CUSTARDS

VANILLA CREAM

✳ Serves 6 ✳ Preparation time 45 minutes ✳ Setting time 4 hours in the fridge

Mrs Beeton gives several recipes for creams and custards in her book, and often these sublimely smooth and delicate little sweets are all you need after a meal. The cream can also be infused with other flavours – bay, angelica or lavender, for example. Experiment and see what you like.

550ml whole milk

60g caster sugar

seeds scraped from
2 vanilla pods

8 egg yolks

3 leaves gelatine

special equipment

a temperature probe and
6 small serving glasses

Place the milk and half the sugar in a small saucepan over a medium heat until warm. Add the vanilla seeds and remove from the heat. Leave for 10 minutes to allow the vanilla to infuse the milk.

Meanwhile, in a large bowl, whisk the egg yolks with the remaining sugar until the mixture is light and creamy and set aside. Now place the gelatine leaves into a bowl of cold water for 10 minutes.

Place the vanilla-infused milk mixture back on the hob over a medium heat and bring it to a simmer. Then pour it, whisking all the while, onto the yolk mixture. Return the entire mixture to the pan and place over a low heat. Stir with a flat wooden spoon or heatproof spatula, ensuring that the mixture cooks but does not curdle. The time it takes to thicken will vary from 5–10 minutes. If you have a temperature probe, use it to monitor the temperature of the mixture until it registers 83°C. At this point quickly strain the mixture through a fine sieve into a cold jug or bowl.

Remove the gelatine sheets from the water and give them a squeeze. Stir them into the warm vanilla mixture until dissolved. Allow the mixture to cool, stirring from time to time, then pour into 6 small serving glasses. Cover each with cling film and chill for 4 hours, or overnight, before serving.

A Note on Gelatine

Gelatine, which is derived from cartilage-rich animal tissues and bones, is the most commonly used setting agent in the kitchen today. Historically, other substances have been used as setting agents, including carageen moss (a seaweed), isinglass (derived from the swim bladders of fish) and agar agar (another seaweed derivative).

Gelatine can be bought in powdered form, but clear, brittle sheet gelatine has a finer flavour, gives a more accurate result and is easier to measure. In the course of testing the recipes for this book, we tested all of the different types of gelatine available. Platinum grade sheets weighing approximately 1.6g each are the best type, and are easy to obtain. Three sheets of this gelatine are sufficient to give a light set to 500ml of jelly served in a glass. If you want to use a mould and will need to turn the jelly out, use four sheets per 500ml.

LEMON POSSET

✳ Serves 6 ✳ Preparation time 5 minutes ✳ Chilling time 1 hour

This is probably the simplest dessert you can make – a flavoured cream that sets with the acidity of the lemon juice. The gelatine helps to stabilise the mixture, which is useful if you want to make it a day ahead, but a light set can be achieved without gelatine.

425ml double cream

125g caster sugar

juice and finely grated zest of 2 large or 3 small lemons

1 leaf gelatine (optional)

special equipment

6 x 120ml ramekins

Place the cream, sugar and lemon zest in a small pan over a low heat. Allow the mixture to simmer for 2 minutes, then remove from the heat.

If you are making the posset a day ahead, soak 1 leaf of gelatine in cold water for at least 10 minutes, squeeze dry and stir into the warm cream mixture at this stage.

Once the cream has cooled to tepid, stir in the lemon juice. Strain into 6 glasses, cover with cling film and put straight into the fridge to chill for at least 1 hour before serving.

ICED VANILLA PARFAIT

✳ Serves 6–8 ✳ Preparation time 30 minutes ✳ Freezing time 4 hours

Mrs Beeton gives lots of recipes for frozen fruit purées, which are made into ice creams with double cream. These are delicious, but fiddly to make at home without an ice cream machine. An alternative recipe is this one for a parfait, which is easier to make and does not require constant stirring once it has been moved to the freezer.

4 egg yolks

seeds scraped from 3 vanilla pods

120g caster sugar

400ml double cream

special equipment

a small loaf tin and a balloon whisk

Line the loaf tin with cling film, leaving some overhanging to cover the parfait when made, and freeze on a level surface.

Place the egg yolks and vanilla seeds into the bowl of an electric mixer fitted with the whisk attachment and whisk at high speed until the yolks are very light and pale and have tripled in volume. Meanwhile, place the sugar and 30ml water into a small pan over a high heat to dissolve the sugar. Let it simmer for 2 mins to make a syrup, but don't let it caramelise. With the mixer still running, steadily pour the hot syrup into the yolks and leave the mixer running until the mixture cools.

Place the cream into a bowl and whisk until it reaches a loose but whipped consistency, just before the soft peak stage. If it is too stiff it will be difficult to incorporate into the egg mixture and you will risk over-mixing it.

When the egg mixture has cooled and is very light and fluffy fold in one-third of the whipped cream, taking care not to lose any air. Then add this mixture back into the bowl with the rest of the cream. Combine thoroughly, using a balloon whisk but mixing as little as possible.

Pour the mixture into the lined loaf tin and cover with the overhanging cling film. Leave to freeze for a minimum of 4 hours, and preferably overnight.

Once it has frozen, turn the parfait out of the loaf tin and wrap it well in plenty of cling film as it will easily take on the flavour of other products in the freezer. Use within 1 month. To serve, unwrap and slice using a knife dipped in hot water.

LEMON CREMET

✳ Serves 4 ✳ Preparation time 20 minutes spread over 2 days

Cooks of Mrs Beeton's era were used to making their own curds and light cheeses – they had to. This recipe demonstrates just how easy it is to turn curds into a delightful summer dessert. Try it with homemade shortbread (see page 60).

1 quantity homemade cream cheese (see page 82)

finely grated zest of 1 lemon

100ml Jersey pouring cream

caster sugar, to sprinkle

350g poached rhubarb, mixed berries or bottled plums (see pages 38 or 33), to serve

Make the cream cheese.

Beat the lemon zest into the cream cheese and then shape it into a mound on a pretty serving dish. Pour over the Jersey cream. Sprinkle with a little caster sugar and serve accompanied by the prepared fruit of your choice.

SEVILLE ORANGE CREAMS

✳ Serves 6 ✳ Preparation time 5 minutes ✳ Cooking time 1 hour plus chilling overnight

This light custard is Mrs Beeton's beautiful way of using Seville oranges, as opposed to just using them for marmalade. Their taste is unique and available for only a couple of months, so make this while you can, in January or February.

2 Seville oranges

1 tbsp orange liqueur or brandy

4 egg yolks

80g caster sugar

600ml double cream

special equipment

6 x 120ml ramekins and a roasting tin

Preheat the oven to 140°C/gas mark 1.

Using a potato peeler, pare a thin layer of rind from the oranges. Place the rind in a pan of water over a high heat and bring to a boil for 15 minutes to soften. Remove from the heat and strain away the water and set the rind aside.

Place the orange liqueur or brandy, egg yolks, half the sugar, all the softened rind and the juice of 1 of the oranges into a jug blender and blend well until you have a fine purée. Transfer to a 1-litre bowl.

Place the cream in a small saucepan over a medium heat, add the remaining sugar and bring to simmering. Pour the hot cream mixture over the blended purée, stirring not whisking. Strain the mixture through a fine sieve into a jug and set aside.

Fill the kettle and bring to a boil. Meanwhile, divide the orange mixture between the ramekins and set them into a roasting tin. Slowly pour the boiling water into the roasting tin to a depth of 3cm. Cover the tin loosely with a sheet of foil and bake for 30 minutes. Lower the oven temperature to 120°C/gas mark ½ and bake for a further 5 minutes, or until the creams are set around the edges of ramekins but still wobble in the centre.

Remove the creams from the roasting tin and leave to cool for a few minutes before chilling, preferably overnight. Serve with shortbread biscuits.

EVERYDAY CUSTARD

✳ Serves 6 ✳ Preparation time 5 minutes ✳ Cooking time 30 minutes including 15 minutes infusing time

This quick recipe uses cornflour to thicken the sauce. It is an economical way of making custard and is perfect for a trifle (see page 59).

1 tbsp cornflour

450ml whole or Jersey milk

80g caster sugar

1 vanilla pod, split lengthways

4 large egg yolks

special equipment

a heatproof glass bowl
and a temperature probe

In a medium-sized bowl, mix the cornflour and just enough milk to make a thin paste. Set this aside and place the remaining milk, half the sugar and the vanilla pod in a pan. Slowly bring to a boil, whisking often to prevent sticking. Once it has boiled, remove the pan from the heat, cover with a lid and leave for 15 minutes to infuse.

Meanwhile, place the eggs yolks and the remaining sugar in a heatproof glass bowl and whisk until pale and fluffy.

Now remove the vanilla pod from the milk and scrape the seeds from the pod back into the pan. Place the pan over a medium heat. When the mixture is simmering, pour it onto the cornflour mixture in the bowl, stir, and then pour it back into the pan. Simmer for 2–3 minutes, still stirring, to cook the sauce. If the sauce still tastes floury at this point, continue cooking on a low heat for another 1–2 minutes.

Beat the egg yolk mixture once more and then pour the simmering sauce onto it, whisking constantly to combine.

Rinse out the milk pan and half fill with hot water. Place over a medium heat and set the bowl of custard mixture on top, making sure that base of the bowl doesn't touch the water. Cook, stirring continuously, until the custard thickens. If you like, test with a temperature probe as you stir. The sauce needs to cook to 80–83°C to thicken. If your notice it curdling at the bottom of the bowl, remove from the heat immediately.

Strain the cooked custard through a sieve into a serving jug or a cold, clean bowl to stop it cooking any further. Either serve immediately or, if using for a trifle, cool the custard, cover with cling film and store in the fridge for up to 3 days.

SPECIAL CUSTARD

* Serves 4 * Preparation time 5 minutes * Cooking time 30 minutes including 20 minutes infusing time

This recipe takes Mrs Beeton's suggestion of using cream instead of milk and gives a luxurious custard that is perfect for a treat. You may find that when you add the hot cream to the eggs it thickens perfectly without requiring further cooking – if not, simply cook out over simmering water as the recipe suggests.

350ml double cream

50g caster sugar

1 vanilla pod, split lengthways

5 egg yolks

special equipment

a medium-sized heatproof glass bowl

Place the cream, half the sugar and the vanilla pod in a small saucepan over a medium heat. When it reaches simmering point, remove the pan from the heat, cover with a lid and leave for 20 minutes to infuse.

While the cream is infusing, whisk the egg yolks and the remaining sugar together in a medium-sized heatproof glass bowl until light and fluffy. Then half-fill another saucepan with hot water and set it over a medium heat.

Once the cream has infused, remove the vanilla pod and, using a small knife, scrape the seeds into the cream. Then return the cream to the heat and bring to a boil. Just as the cream begins to rise up the sides of the pan, give the eggs a whisk and pour the cream over them, beating to blend the mixture well. Then place the bowl over the pan of water, making sure that the base of the bowl does not touch the water. Stir until the custard thickens. If the sauce begins to curdle, remove it from the heat immediately. Pour the custard through a sieve into a cold, clean bowl or jug and serve.

Note: Sauces that are thickened with egg yolks need to be heated to allow the yolks to coagulate, but overheating causes the mixture to curdle. To avoid this, custards are usually finished in a bowl over a pan of gently simmering water, which can take time. To speed up the process, you can use a microwave. Once the hot cream or milk has been added to the yolks, microwave the mixture in 30-second blasts, stirring well after each to check the thickness of the liquid.

CHEESE &
PRESERVES

EATING AND SERVING CHEESE

If you buy good cheese, eat it as nature intended to enjoy its true flavour. When serving a cheese course as part of a meal, put together a cheeseboard of no more than perhaps two or three perfectly ripe cheeses. These can be served with a combination of oatcakes or other cheese biscuits, bread (nut or fruit versions work well), nuts, fruit and celery – whatever harmonises with the flavour and texture of the cheese. In this chapter you will also find two recipes for fruit preserves, known as cheeses (see pages 82 and 86). Fruit cheese is an excellent foil to the richness of milk cheeses.

BRITISH AND IRISH CHEESES

There are more excellent cheeses made in the British Isles now than probably at any point in our history – and they rightly take their place among the best in the world, thanks to a new generation of farmers and cheese-makers who have revolutionised the industry in recent years.

In Mrs Beeton's time, many large Victorian houses were built with their own dairy and cheese rooms. These were lined with marble and slate, and people made their own dairy products there. Those who did buy dairy products did so mostly from small, farm-based dairies. The majority of cheeses were consumed locally and so few cheeses – Stilton and Cheddar being two notable exceptions – were known beyond their local markets. At a time when refrigeration was only just being developed, the quality of the finished product can only have been variable.

A combination of the nineteenth-century decline in the real value of agricultural wages, rural depression and two World Wars, along with the industrialisation of food production, very nearly killed off any remnants of cheese production as a business. Still, makers of fine cheese persisted and continued to thrive, thanks to the demand for good food.

Significant in the development of modern British cheeses are people such as the cheese-maker and teacher James Aldridge, who was active in the 1980s and 90s, and cheesemonger Randolph Hodgson, who is still chairman of Neal's Yard Dairy today. These two men, along with the authors who publicised the renaissance in the making and appreciation of cheese, have done more than anyone to encourage new cheese-makers to strive for perfection.

It is impossible to describe all of the new cheeses that have appeared on the market in recent years, let alone the land they spring from and the people who produce them. A few popular national favourites are listed (see opposite). You can find contact details of cheese suppliers at the back of the book.

Hard cheeses

Isle of Mull Cheddar – unpasteurised cows'-milk cheese, Isle of Mull, Scotland.
The grandest of strong Cheddars with a smooth, almost fudgy, texture and a lovely
fruity, farmyard tang

Keen's Cheddar – unpasteurised cows'-milk cheese, Wincanton, Somerset.
A firm, nutty Cheddar with a long flavour and good bite at the end

Gorwydd Caerphilly – unpasteurised cows'-milk cheese, Llandewi Brefi, Wales.
A cheese of contrasting flavours and textures – citric, lactic and earthy – all balanced together

Cornish Yarg – pasteurised cows'-milk cheese, Pengreep, Cornwall.
A crumbly but moist cheese with delicate, sweet dairy notes

St Gall – unpasteurised cows'-milk cheese, Fermoy, County Cork.
A very smooth-textured cheese with long, creamy and nutty flavours

Ticklemore – pasteurised goats'-milk cheese, Sharpham Estate, Devon.
Lovely fresh, lactic flavours and a light, crumbly texture

Soft cheeses

Childwickbury – pasteurised goats'-milk cheese, St Albans, Hertfordshire.
Delicate, fresh, young cheese with a light, smooth texture and sharp milky flavour

St Tola – unpasteurised goats'-milk cheese, Inagh, County Clare.
A luxurious cheese with a light texture and a rich, creamy, sometimes floral, flavour

Tymsboro – unpasteurised goats'-milk cheese, Timsbury, Somerset.
Full-flavoured, creamy goat cheese

Clava – pasteurised cows'-milk cheese, Ardersier, Inverness.
A creamy, brie-like cheese with a flavour that is full and deep, but lacking the bite of French brie

Ardrahan – pasteurised cows'-milk cheese, Kanturk, County Cork.
A semi-soft cheese with a buttery texture. The washed rind has a delightfully pungent aroma, which
provides the perfect contrast to the delicate, nutty flavour of the cheese

Elmhirst – unpasteurised cows'-milk cheese from the 60-year-old Sharpham Jersey herd,
Sharpham Estate, Devon.
A rich, triple-cream cheese with a surprisingly light texture and flavour that develops as the
cheese matures

Blue cheeses

Colston Bassett Stilton – pasteurised cows'-milk cheese, Colston Bassett, Nottinghamshire.
A rich, buttery-textured cheese with a balanced fruity and savoury mineral flavour

Beenleigh Blue – pasteurised ewes'-milk cheese, Ashprington, Devon.
A beautiful, rich, clean-tasting blue

Strathdon Blue – pasteurised cows'-milk cheese, Tain, Ross-shire.
A smooth, pale-blue cheese with a salty yet well-balanced milky flavour

Cornish Blue – Liskeard, Cornwall.
A young blue cows'-milk cheese with a sweet, mild and creamy flavour and a soft, giving texture

Stichelton – unpasteurised organic cows'-milk cheese, Welbeck Estate, Nottinghamshire.
A firm but silky texture with long, complex flavours of spice and sugar

Yorkshire Blue – pasteurised cows'-milk cheese, Newsham, North Yorkshire.
A soft, creamy, blue-veined cheese with a sweet, buttery flavour but lacking the bite of traditional blue cheeses

FRESH CREAM CHEESE

✳ Serves 4 ✳ Preparation time 10 minutes ✳ Cooking time 10 minutes

This delicately flavoured cheese is easy to make and luscious served with summer berries. Alternatively, use it in sweet and savoury recipes, like the lemon cremet on page 70.

325ml single cream

325ml milk

100ml buttermilk or live yoghurt

¾ tsp rennet or vegetable rennet

caster sugar, for sprinkling

Put the cream and milk in a large pan and warm gently until hand-hot. Remove from the heat, add the buttermilk or live yoghurt, and the rennet and leave in a warm place until set.

Line a sieve with some muslin and place over a large bowl. Spoon the mixture into the sieve, cover and chill for 4–5 hours or overnight. During this time the whey will drain from the cheese and can be discarded.

Transfer the curds to a dish and serve sprinkled with caster sugar and accompanied by Jersey cream and fresh fruit compote or bottled fruit (see page 33) on the side.

BLACKCURRANT CHEESE

✳ Makes 750g – about 3 or 4 jars ✳ Preparation time 10 minutes ✳ Cooking time 30 minutes

In the style of Mrs Beeton, this preserve is included to use up the remains of the blackcurrant cordial recipe on page 20. Richly flavoured, it can be served with terrines or cheeses, or simply cut it into chunks, dipped in caster sugar and enjoyed as a sweet.

800g blackcurrants – or you can use the pulp discarded after making blackcurrant cordial (see page 20). In this case, use only 400g sugar.

600g jam sugar

special equipment

a large stainless steel preserving pan

Place your jars on a clean baking sheet in a low oven at 120°C/gas mark ½. Purée the fruit thoroughly in a food processor, then pass through a fine sieve into a large stainless steel pan. Add the sugar, and cook over a medium heat, stirring constantly, until a rapid boil is achieved, then reduce the heat to low and cook until the mixture thickens and a spoon drawn across the bottom of the pan leaves a clean trail. This will take approximately 15–20 minutes.

Pot the cheese into your sterilised jars, cover the surface of the cheese with a waxed-paper disc and seal with cellophane. Store in a cool, dark place and use within 1 year of making.

WELSH RAREBIT

✳ Serves 4 ✳ Preparation time 10 minutes ✳ Cooking time 10 minutes

A simple, tasty way to serve hot cheese, this recipe serves as a useful reminder that once we used to eat savouries after dessert, or in place of it. Mrs Beeton recommends the use of little heated dishes to help keep the cheese warm – in a modern kitchen we have the advantage of a grill under which we can heat the mixture to bubbling perfection.

200g Isle of Mull Cheddar, or other strong cheese, grated

1 medium egg

50ml milk or beer

½ tsp English mustard powder

1 tbsp Worcestershire sauce, plus extra to serve

freshly ground black pepper

4 large slices bread

Place the grated cheese into a large bowl. Add the egg, milk or beer, mustard powder and Worcestershire sauce. Grind over some black pepper and mix well together.

Turn the grill on to high and toast each slice of bread on one side. Spread the cheese mixture onto the untoasted side of the bread and place the slices back under the grill, cheese-side up, not less than 10cm from the grill element. Let it cook until golden and bubbling. Remove from the heat and sprinkle with extra Worcestershire sauce, to taste. This is lovely served with tomato chutney.

DAMSON CHEESE

✳ Makes 1.8kg – 4 or 5 jars ✳ Preparation time 30 minutes ✳ Cooking time 1 hour 30 minutes

Mrs Beeton gave several recipes for fruit cheeses, which are really only cooked fruit pastes. This is a long-keeping preserve that is ideal served as a condiment with cheese.

1.5kg damsons

200ml water

approx 1–1½kg preserving or granulated sugar

2 tbsp lemon juice

special equipment

a large stainless steel preserving pan and a small hammer

Pick over the fruit, removing debris and leaves and discarding any bruised or damaged fruit, then place in a large stainless steel pan. Bring to a simmer over a low to medium heat. Turn the heat down low and simmer uncovered until the stones easily come away from the fruit and the damsons break down completely. Stir occasionally to prevent the fruit sticking to the bottom of the pan and catching. This will take around 30 minutes, depending on the ripeness of the fruit.

Put the cooked fruit through a fine sieve, reserving the stones. Pick out 30 stones and crack each with a small hammer. You will see a small brown kernel inside. Peel and remove the white flesh inside, chop the kernels finely and add to the pulp. You should end up with about 1.2kg.

When you are ready to finish the cheese, place your clean jars on a baking sheet in a cool oven, 120°C/gas mark ½.

Weigh the sieved pulp and add the same weight of sugar. Place both these ingredients in the pan, stirring over a low heat to dissolve the sugar. It is faster to finish the pulp in two batches, so remove half to a large bowl and continue to cook the portion that remains in the pan. Turn the heat up to medium and cook, stirring constantly with a heatproof spatula or flat wooden spoon, until a rapid boil is achieved. Reduce the heat to low and cook until the mixture thickens and a spoon drawn across the bottom of the pan leaves a clean trail. This will take approximately 15–20 minutes.

Pot the first batch of cheese into the sterilised jars, and then finish the second batch. Cover the surface of the cheese with a waxed-paper disc and seal the jar with cellophane. Store in a cool, dark place and use within 1 year.

DIGESTIFS

ORANGE BRANDY

❋ Makes approx 1.5 litres ❋ Preparation time 5 minutes plus 7 days steeping

The Seville orange is largely produced for the British market because we never lost our desire for making Seville orange marmalade (see *Mrs Beeton Cakes & Bakes*). However, during the short period of time Seville oranges are available here in January and February, you can also use them for making Mrs Beeton's delectable orange brandy, which can be served on its own or poured over ice.

zest of 3 Seville oranges

200ml Seville orange juice (approximately 6–7 oranges)

1 litre brandy

400g caster sugar

special equipment

a 1.5-litre Kilner or preserving jar, a sieve lined with muslin and a tinted bottle with a screw cap

Using a potato peeler, remove the peel from the oranges and place it in the bottom of the jar. Add the juice, brandy and sugar, then stir well and seal the jar. Stir daily over the next 7 days then strain through a sieve lined with muslin into a jug for ease of pouring. Pour the orange brandy into a bottle and seal. Store the bottle in a cool, dark place for 1 month before using.

To serve, add a dessertspoonful of the brandy to a glass of English sparkling wine for a delightful aperitif, or pour it over ripe strawberries for a fruity treat.

BRAMBLE LIQUEUR

✳ Makes approx 1.2 litres ✳ Preparation time 5 minutes plus 2 months steeping

This marvellous liqueur takes its inspiration from Mrs Beeton's whiskey cordial and exemplifies her pleasure in taking simple ingredients and creating something special with them. Replacing the whiskey with a more neutral vodka or gin allows the flavour of the fruit to dominate. This fruit combination captures the glossy, purple-black allure of fresh wild blackberries, but the recipe also works with other fruits, such as sloes or wild damsons: just prick them all over before immersing them in the alcohol. Storing the finished liqueur in tinted bottles helps to stop the colour fading.

800g ripe brambles, picked over to remove any debris

200g caster sugar

600ml vodka or gin

special equipment

a 1.2-litre Kilner or preserving jar, a sieve lined with muslin and 2–3 tinted bottles with screw caps

Pack the brambles into the jar and add the sugar, shaking so that it sifts down and fills the gaps between the fruit. Pour in the vodka or gin and seal.

Keep in a cool, dark place for 2 months. For the first 7 days give the jar a shake once a day.

After 2 months strain the liqueur through a sieve lined with muslin into a jug for ease of pouring. Pour the liqueur into bottles and seal. Use within 1 year of making.

PRODUCERS & SUPPLIERS

Cheese and dairy

George Mews Cheese

106 Byres Road, Glasgow G12 8TB

Tel 0141 334 5900

www.georgemewescheese.co.uk

George has a carefully balanced selection of world-class British and European artisan cheeses.

Moorlands Cheesemakers

Lorien House, South Street, Castle Cary, Somerset BA7 7ES

Tel 0196 335 0634

www.cheesemaking.co.uk

Katrin Loxton sells everything you need to make your own cheeses at home, from various forms of rennet and cultures to complete cheesemaking kits.

Neal's Yard Dairy

108 Druid Street, London SE1 2HH

Tel 020 7500 7520

www.nealsyarddairy.co.uk

Neal's Yard buy and mature cheese from about seventy cheesemakers on farms around Britain and Ireland. They sell the cheese to shops and restaurants all over the world, and to the public from their two shops in London.

Paxton and Whitfield

93 Jermyn Street, London SW1Y 6JE

Tel 020 7930 0259

www.paxtonandwhitfield.co.uk

One of the most respected cheesemongers in the country, with a long established history in fine cheese retailing.

PGT Hook & Son

Longleys Farm, Harebeating Lane, Hailsham, East Sussex BN27 1ER

Tel: 0132 344 9494

www.hookandson.co.uk

Hook & Son supply extremely natural, unpasteurised milk, cream and butter from their sustainably managed cows. They offer a mail order service from their website.

Useful organisations

FARMA

Lower Ground Floor, 12 Southgate Street, Winchester, Hampshire SO23 9EF

Tel 0845 458 8420

www.farmersmarkets.net

FARMA represents the sale of local food and fresh farm products direct to the public through farmers' markets and farm shops. Visit their website for a list of certified markets and suppliers in your area.

Freedom Food Limited

Wilberforce Way, Southwater, Horsham, West Sussex RH139RS

Tel 0300 123 0014

www.rspca.org.uk/freedomfood

The RSPCA's farm assurance and food labelling scheme is the only UK scheme to focus solely on improving the welfare of farm animals reared for food.

Slow Food UK

Slow Food UK, 6 Neal's Yard, Covent Garden, London WC2H 9DP

Tel 020 7099 1132

www.slowfood.org.uk

Join thousands of members and discover connections with local groups around the UK that link the pleasure of artisan food to community and the environment.

Soil Association

South Plaza, Marlborough Street, Bristol BS1 3NX

Tel 0117 314 5000

www.soilassociation.org

The Soil Association is a charity campaigning for planet-friendly food and farming. It offers guidance to consumers looking for local suppliers of organic food as well as advice for organic growers and businesses.

GLOSSARY OF COOKING TERMS

Many languages have influenced the British kitchen, but none so much as French – hardly surprising since French food has often been held up as the benchmark for excellence, in Mrs Beeton's time as well as in our own. Long before the Michelin guide began to report on British restaurants, French chefs were working for British royalty and could be found in the kitchens of many large country houses. Perhaps the most famous of these was Antonin Carême, chef to the Prince Regent (later George IV), who set the standard for future chefs to emulate. Mrs Beeton knew of him by name and reputation. The list below is intended to help explain the more commonly used terms – many, but not all, of which come from the French.

agar-agar   a vegetable setting agent made from seaweed

bain marie   a large pan or tin used as a waterbath to cook or warm food that is too delicate to withstand direct heat

baking powder   a raising agent made from bicarbonate of soda and cream of tartar

beat   to mix food energetically to introduce air, using a wooden spoon, whisk or electric mixer to make a mixture light and fluffy

butter muslin   a fine cotton cloth used for straining jellies, stocks and dairy products. It should be scalded before use.

caramel   a confection made by melting sugar. A simple caramel can be made by gently warming a mixture of sugar and water to 170–180°C, until the sugar melts and turns golden brown

chill   to cool food without freezing, usually in a refrigerator

clafoutis   a baked batter pudding made with fruit, often cherries (see page 28)

cocotte   a small dish in which eggs, mousses and souffles are baked

coeur à la crème   a heart-shaped mould of cream or curd cheese

compote   a dish of stewed fruit in sugar syrup, served cold

conserve   a sweet preserve usually made with whole fruits

consistency   texture, used to describe cakes and doughs

cornflour   the ground kernels of corn/maize, used for thickening liquids and sauces

couverture   chocolate made especially for cooking, which contains a high proportion of cocoa butter. It has a glossier appreareance and is easier to handle than standard chocolate

crimp   to press pastry together decoratively, to seal

curd   the solids left after milk is soured, following the removal of the whey

curdling   the process whereby fresh milk or sauce separates into solids and liquid. This can be intentional, as when making cheese, or unfortunate – for example when creamed butter and sugar split with the addition of eggs

dough   a mixture of flour, liquid and sometimes fat for baking into bread or cakes

dredge   to sprinkle food with flour or sugar

dumpling   a small ball of dough or stuffing that is steamed or poached, and often served with soup or stews

dust   to sprinkle lightly, for example with flour, sugar or spices

emulsion   a suspension of tiny droplets of one liquid in another liquid

fold in   to combine ingredients carefully with a whisk, metal spoon or spatula in order to retain any air that has been incorporated into the mixutre

fool   a dessert of whipped cream or custard folded with fruit purée

fromage blanc   a light, soft curd cheese

gelatine   a setting agent derived from the bones of animals, used for setting jellies

glaze   a glossy finish given to food, usually by brushing with beaten egg or milk before cooking, or with sugar syrup after cooking

gluten   the main protein component of some flours, notably wheat flours

hull to remove the green calyx from fruits such as strawberries or raspberries

infuse to combine aromatic flavourings with a liquid such as milk or stock (or, in the case of tea making, water) and leave them for a period of time to impart their flavour

jelly a liquid set with gelatine or another gelling agent

macerate to soften food, often fruit, by adding sugar

maslin pan jam pan

meringue a light mixture of beaten egg whites and sugar

molasses the liquid that remains once sugar has been crystallised

nibbed (of nuts, usually almonds) chopped

parfait a chilled or frozen dessert

pasty an oval-shaped pastry case with savoury or sweet filling

pectin a gum-like substance which acts as a setting agent in jams and jellies. It is found naturally in some fruits and vegetables, notably lemons

pith the bitter white tissue that is found inside the rind of citrus fruits

poach to cook food in simmering liquid

pulp the soft, fleshy tissue of fruit or vegetables, or the result of cooking or mashing fruit

purée food that has been blended or passed through a sieve to give a smooth texture

ramekin a small ceramic, ovenproof dish, often used for soufflés or creams

reduce to concentrate a liquid, for example a sauce or stock, by boiling it until a portion has evaporated

rennet a substance extracted from the stomach lining of calves. It is used to coagulate milk for junket, and for making cheese

sabayon a light, beaten mixture of egg yolks or whole eggs and sugar

setting point the stage of cooking a jam or jelly at which it will set when cooled

sift to pass flour or sugar through a sieve to remove any lumps and/or incorporate air

simmer to cook in liquid that is kept just below boiling point

skim to remove residue from the surface of a liquid, for example fat from stock or scum from jam

soufflé a baked dish consisting of a sauce or purée, usually thickened with egg yolks and lightened with beaten egg whites, which rises during cooking

spring-form describes a cake tin with hinged sides and a loose bottom

steam to cook food in the steam that rises from a pan of boiling water

steep to soak in liquid, in order to hydrate

stir to mix with a circular motion, using a spoon or fork

strain to separate liquids from solids by passing through a sieve or muslin

syrup a sugar dissolved in water or another liquid

vanilla sugar sugar with a vanilla flavour, usually made by storing caster sugar with used vanilla pods in order to extract the oils

whey the liquid part of milk that is left after the curds have been removed in the process of cheese making

whip to beat eggs or cream until they are thick and increased in volume

whisk a looped wire utensil that is used to introduce air into ingredients such as eggs or cream

yeast a fungus used to leaven bread

zest the coloured outer skin of citrus fruits in which the highly flavoured oils are contained

INDEX

ACKNOWLEDGEMENTS

Mum, Sandra Baker, helped without question in the kitchen and office both in the process of testing the recipes and in organising manuscripts – you are a blessing.

To my sister Louise, and to Oscar and Fanny for providing moral support go hearty thanks. Much respect and love goes to Dad, John Baker.

My great friend, Joyce Molyneux taught me delicacy and restraint in addition to a love of seasonal, simple puddings. Adam Sellar provided great support in the kitchen during the testing of the recipes – thank you.

Amanda Harris and Debbie Woska sat through the creation of Mrs Beeton *How to Cook* with me – providing just the right amount of support and encouragement – thank you.

Zelda Turner deserves thanks for helping trim and sculpt the recipes in this smaller collection.

To all the design team – Julyan Bayes, Lucie Steriker, Sammy-Jo Squire and her crew, and the photographer Andrew Hayes-Watkins and his team for making the book look so beautiful. The team behind the scenes at Orion helped enormously – Elizabeth Allen and Nicky Carswell especially.

Gerard Baker

COUNDON